Embers of the fire

r.j. blonde

To my mom, dad and sons.

ISBN 978-1-7328169-9-2 (Paperback Edition)

Book design by R.J. Blonde
Illustrations by iStock
Published by R.J. Blonde

love

I want to be–
every thought,
every day,
everywhere,
every pulse of your heart,
deep within your soul–
to never be,
let go.

The eyes smile when you're in love.

The light in my mind,
is shining brighter,
than the stars,
in the night's sky.

There is a lightness
to my being,
like angels,
resting on my soul.

When you're high on love,
remember how hard you fall.

r.j.

I dance sometimes on moonbeams,
and float from star to star,
then tiptoe by the moonlight,
to get to where you are.

The night is calling me
to dance to the rhythm
of my heart until it
takes my breath away.

Shh!
Be still,
so I can hear the echo of your love,
as does the nightingale,
calling out in the dark,
of night.

Be still my heart–just breathe for me.

I thought I knew what love was–the flutter of the heart, the continuous smile on ones face. Excitement in the voice. The kiss that never ends. All the replays of the mind I go over and over it. Truth is? I don't know what true love is. I've tried two times and failed to have love last. Is it me or them or both? I don't know that either. I'm now too tired to even try again. I didn't think I knew true love, but I do. The love of a child and the love of a mother. Truer love has never been. And that love, will never fail.

Love runs through my veins,
'til my heart can pump,
no more.

I want you near me,
to bury myself,
in your heart–
to listen to the rhythm of your love,
'til death do us part.

I want to move on,
but my heart–
refuses to go.

There is a glow in my mind.

I can see, yet cannot find.

Is this glow just for me?

Or, can other people see?

I will follow this for sure,

maybe I can cure.

I'm here.

I can see that glow,

and now I am,

for I know,

that what I now see,

are the crystal tears,

of me.

I'm the rose,
in the center of your
bouquet of life.
You need to make it
through the wildflowers,
before you find
that special one.

Kiss me awake,
like the morning dew–
leave love droplets,
on me too.

I lay down to the moon,
to sleep with no fear,
and arise to the sun,
just to feel you near.

Love yourself–

listen to your mind sing.

Go ahead–
chase the rainbows,
you may just find,
your pot of gold.

I know in my past I pushed you away,
kind of afraid you would not stay.
I've kept you at a distance for years,
but now I don't fear,
you are here to stay,
closer than near.
And by myself,
I found you right here,
the real me can now shout and cheer.
I hope I'm blessed for years,
and hold me dear.

I dream while I'm awake,
this is how,
I escape.

I'm in love,

so happy I found you,

I've waited forever,

thought I would never,

but now,

it will do.

It's like love,

is ready to live it through.

Let me lay beside your
dream so I may come true.

I'm like a sunflower,
ready to bloom–
just need some sunshine,
to see me through.

I'm dancing on moonbeams,
to get where you are,
then I'll be the brightest,
in your galaxy of stars.

Kiss me and you'll wish I was yours,
forever.

I would write a love story,
except I'm missing one of the
main characters–
you and your love.

I wish I could hold your
heart like you hold mine.

Love yourself first–
that's the only true love,
you'll ever have.

Raindrops hitting my skin,
reminds me of the passion,
I felt in our love.

Come lay beside me,
so I can wrap you up,
in me.

At the window of our love,

wearing nothing but moonbeams,

that light your path to me.

I am standing
in the doorway of your heart,
hoping to open your love.

As I lay my head on your
chest, I hear the whisper
of your heart, that brings
me such peace, and
makes me love you more.

I want to see your galaxy,
like you see the stars,
in my eyes.

I have many faults,
one I know for sure,
I love to much and trust me,
there's no cure.

You are the light,
in the darkness of my soul.

A rose is a symbol of love.

A red rose to celebrate that feeling is
the color of the blood that pumps from
the heart. Blooms out its petals like love
grows from within. One day, you see
the color fading and a darkness covers
those petals. A stem once bright green, is
turning brown and discarding, the leaves
of life. All is gone but the thorns of pain
to never allow the beauty to be. All has
withered away to the darkness of never.

My heart is singing love
songs to the emptiness.

I wish I did not love too much,
but it's just how I roll,
let me tell you that kind of love,
will surely take its toll.

Don't sit near me!
I'm contagious!
You'll get the love bug,
and it's very hard to cure.

Every day we are reborn–
open your heart,
and celebrate you.

You are my forever–
forever you are.

My heart and soul are so very kind,
yet my eyes have become,
increasingly blind,
trying to see if love exists for me,
of any kind.

loss

I put it away when we met.

Through time I forgot about it.

For years it never came to mind.

One day, you decided to walk away.

I was alone–truly alone after years with you.

Now what do I do?

I lost you.

Where do I turn now.

Where did it go?

I must dig deep to find it.

I don't remember.

Will I ever find it again?

Every day, piece by broken piece,

I begin to find it.

It's hard to put it back the way it was.

In time, I found it.

It's me!

I found me–never to lose me again,

in another.

She put every breath she took into you,
while you blew her life away.

Around in circles,
when will it stop,
I'm dizzy from heartache,
I may just drop.
Someone please tell me,
how long it will be,
before I'm okay
and back to me?

My mind is bleeding,
with thoughts of heartache.

I cry,

I cry,

to the stars in the darkened sky.

Why?

Just why,

do I still cry?

Don't let someone
awaken your sleeping
heart to destroy your soul.

Do I ever creep into your mind?
Do I ever make you wonder?
Did you really ever love me?
Did you really ever care about me?
I think I can answer them all–
No!
I realize if any of this were true,
you would have fought to keep me and
the marriage together.
Now I see,
even with my eyes closed,
'no' is still my answer.

Are you there?

I can't see.

Why are you running away from me?

Oh go!

Just go!

I don't want to know.

You were loved like never before.

Oh go!

Just go!

Close the door.

I don't love you anymore.

Never lose yourself in another.
Sometimes it takes heartbreak,
to find you.

I've become a sponge,
absorbing all the hurt I can,
no one will squeeze the life from me,
again.

I wish they made a cleanser,
so I could wash you from my mind.

I dig and dig,

it's not just a hole,

a grave so deep,

it goes to my soul.

I'm having a wake,

to celebrate the day,

I fill that grave,

so you will go away.

The person I loved,

no longer to see,

maybe my feelings,

are buried,

with thee.

Someday,
I hope to see happiness in
the reflection of my eyes.

My words are deafening
to the deafening silence.

A sadness is washing over me,
drowning me in tears,
like waves crashing the rocks at sea.

Let me count the ways I still love you–

zero.

I am weak,
then I am strong,
that's when everybody,
takes me wrong.

I wish I could escape
the silence of your words.

I run, sob and scream,

it chases me in my dreams.

Never leaves me,

even when I stare.

My daily nightmare,

those feelings,

that I care.

I loved you hard,
you set my world on fire,
then you walked away,
and left me scarred.

The pain is good.
It's teaching me not to care.

Go ahead,
play games with life,
but as you move the pieces around
your board just remember–
you will someday land,
on reality.

A soulmate is something special some never find. I thought I had, 'til he walked out, and left me behind.

The ashes of fire that once was a love,
will burn you,
like the embers of the fire.

I'm tired of trying to be,
everything people want out of me.
It's hard sometimes for me to smile,
even if it's only for awhile.
It's an act I'm trying to work through,
because I wanted nothing but love,
from you.

My mind is flooded with tears
from my broken heart.

Love doesn't understand me.

Every day,

every hour,

every minute,

every second,

I get closer to the day,

where the hurt,

goes away.

I'm living a nightmare in my awake.

I wish I could protect
my heart from the storm
engulfing my mind.

Sometimes the real in someone,
fakes us out.

In the darkness of my mind,
I see the heartache,
of my life.

I tried to wipe love from my heart,
but the memories,
are still there to haunt me.

Oh heart!
Please stop skipping beats,
and walk away.

I will cry no more,

you hurt me to the core.

I loved you so deep,

it's robbed me from my sleep.

I won't go on taking blame,

it was you who were playing,

the game.

You were like the man on the moon–
that far away from reality.

I am better now,
I am on the mend.
No, I cannot be your friend.
I love myself not being blue.
Now I am not sorry,
you are you.

My eyes flutter open,
I see you standing there,
I reach to touch you,
then realize your not there.
It was just my heartache,
floating in the air.

Don't awaken the devil in me,
you may release your hell.

My heart will forever haunt you,
because my heart is yours,
no more.

Sometimes,
it's so dark,
sitting in the light.

Happily ever afters
only apply to fairytales.

There's not enough
makeup to cover up
a broken heart.

The fight inside me,
is a war that never ends.

No one here,
no one there,
no one around me,
anywhere.

My tears remind me of morning dew,
dripping down to the core,
of me and you.

Trust me,
someday,
I will make YOU cry.

Looking out the window,
the sun glistens off my tears,
because I finally realize,
I wasted all those years.

I am living in the shadows of
a broken heart that takes no
sunshine to appear.

Follow my teardrops,
and you will find,
a shattered dream,
and a broken heart.

You have broken my spirit,
but not my wings,
I will fly above the storm clouds,
to a beautiful life ahead.

I have built these walls around me,
one painful thought at a time,
to shield my heart from the pain,
of '*so called love.*'

It hurts to walk the path
of shattered dreams.

Tears slowly run down my body,
until I'm wrapped in the grief,
of our love.

Can I ever love with such
passion as I once felt?
Will I become as one
with another?

I feel so alone around people.

I hide the tears,

in the sweat of my brow,

so no one can see,

the pain.

I thought a change in my life,
would change my life,
but it only changed,
where I am.

I sit in silence,
crying out inside for my heartbreak,
to heal.

My silence screams–'*listen*'.

I am walking away from
the pain you left behind.

I gave you my soul,
and you tossed it away,
like an old pair of shoes.

I am lost to you.

I used to have this,
I carried it for years,
it gave me such joy,
but now just tears.
All my life I look forward to this in time,
because I just knew it would be all mine.
Now that I'm old,
it has gone cold,
my dreams mean nothing to me,
I'm just old.

My mind is tired from trying
to protect my heart.

My heart could explode from anger,
but that would only kill me.

The wall around my heart,
is strong enough to take it,
so please,
stop trying to break it.

What will this day bring to me?
I really wish I had the key.
I'm feeling a little down today,
I don't know why I feel this way.
I look and see no change for me.
My heart is still hurt,
but no one can see.

life

Sometimes,
I can close my eyes and feel the soft-
ness of my mom's cheek when I would
kiss her goodbye. I can even see me
and her on the front porch when I
would do that. It takes me back to a
special time–a time I will never forget.

We all have storage in a special place
in our hearts for those who mean or
meant the world to us. It's my secret
place that I am the only one who goes
there. It's a storage place, of love.

The passion for life is
fluttering like the pulse
of a new adventure.

The pain of yesterday,
gives me the strength of today,
and the power,
to get through tomorrow.

Age gave her wisdom,
in the wrinkles of time.

I'm a warrior,

through and through,

and fight battles because of you.

I'm stronger than ever,

with the strength of two,

don't come to my door,

you'll be sorry if you do.

Exercise your life,
just be careful,
adding poundage.

I feel like a new butterfly,
beginning to spread it's wings,
for life's first flight.

I lay here in the silent dark of night.

I have no fear.

My heart is pounding oh so loud,

I can hear.

The sounds of darkness,

are so very near.

I lay here not afraid of the night.

There is truly no fright.

Just the deafening sound,

of an empty night,

that feels right.

I give you food for thought–

as you get older, your dreams fade.

Mine did.

I'm sure I'm not alone.

When you're young, that is always with you.

Some of you are lucky to accomplish your dreams.

Others like me, never had that chance, because my

partners were not with me about my dreams.

Now I'm too old to dream.

I know you need to still have them, but they change.

I guess I kind of have them, but they are not about

richers, or big homes, or fancy cars.

Now it's about waking up every day,

seeing the sunrise and set.

Breathing in the joy of still being here.

Feeling blessed and accomplishment,

to just be alive.

Being with your family and knowing their love.

Enjoy your days and thank god for every second,

minute, and hour of all the days of your life.

That's what you dream about when you get old.

Dreams do come true.

In the shadows of my heart,
I can feel time ticking away.
My life has changed so much,
it gets better every day.
Life has come full circle,
now it's my time to play!

Our bodies are like a canvas,
waiting for one stroke of life at a time.

I've been clawing my way up,
like a person buried alive by others,
until I finally saw the light,
and began to see,
me.

Life is good,
life is bad,
life is happy,
life is sad,
life goes on all these ways,
'til life is no more,
so seize this day.

The hands of time move swiftly with age,
only you can slow them down,
'til one strike of the clock,
is left.

We are actors in life.

If you think about it, no one really knows you–sometimes you don't know who you really are. We all have our ways we cope or live, that only we can make our life better. You can never depend on another to make you. Only you can do that. Be true to you.

We tend to make ourselves,
judge and jury,
and find ourselves,
forever guilty.

Today is the day,
I can look forward to tomorrow.

I am free to be me.

Turn your pain into
gaining your life back.

My life as a story is a journey of love–I thought.

Alone for awhile, love again–I thought–alone again.
So many mistakes. So many lessons. Some learned,
some repeated. All lessons are not learned from.
Why do we always think we are to blame for
failures? I think we fail ourselves by allowing others
to take over our hearts and minds. I've been told
'I'm so strong.' Oh, if they could only be in my mind
and heart. We are great actresses to the outside
world. Then collapse behind closed doors. So many
tears, so much thoughts of hurt and pain to only
see the moon through our watery eyes, blinking to
see the sunrise. Lack of sleep, but the show must
go on. Everyone says, time heals. No it doesn't.
When you're older, you don't have a lot of time to
heal. You just go on. Put on the face of joy with a
heavy heart and that never ending questions: why?
The sad part is, you will never know, which makes it
harder. No rest for the heart or mind, just diversions
of the day-to-day, with the hope this weight of life
becomes a little less every sunrise.

Believe in yourself,
No one else will.

We all have the power within ourselves.

Dwelling on the past will
only confuse the future.

I feel sometimes deep in my soul,
that no love is there,
for me to know.
I'm happy where I am in life,
but sometimes I feel,
the blade of a knife.
Cutting my heart in two,
knowing I really wanted my love,
to stay for you.
But it's slowly slipping away,
each and every day.

As the sunrises,

it appears again.

It stays with me wherever I go.

I wish I could catch it,

but I know it will fade.

It's so dark as the day wears on.

Then as the sun sets,

and darkness appears,

it escapes into me,

and with that there's no fear.

Because it's the shadow of me,

as I used to appear.

I have fought hard from the deepest
depth to retrieve my power.
I will not give up.
I am my own warrior.
And will continue,
to charge.

Is there truth hidden in some lies?

Or are there lies,

hidden in some truths?

Look them in the eye,
say what you mean,
stop hiding behind
your emotional screen.

I will dance to my own music,
and sing my own songs.

I walk through life,
like it's a garden of flowers.
sometimes,
not so lightly,
and stomp my way through.

My eyes see the
brightness through the
darkness of my mind.

Since you finally set me free,
I'm getting back,
to me.

I'm not alone, but I'm lonely. I'm sad, but you see no tears. I'm smiling, but not happy. I'm laughing, but I'm hurting. I'm old, but my heart is young. I'm alive, but not living. I'm looking in my mirror, but do not see. I'm changing, but you can't see. I can't help but just be me. You don't know me, because you can't see.

I'm looking at my reflection,
in the pool of tears I've shed,
that really isn't me now,
that person I see is dead.

I am hungry for life,
slowly filling up my plate.

Everyone wants revenge,
but silence,
is the best we can give.

Bury the hurt,
before the hurt,
buries you.

They say we learn from our past,
Then why do we keep them in the present?

There is a sound, a sound we hear
louder and louder as the years go by.
When young, it is just a whisper, but as
the days go by and we grow we hear it
only slightly louder. It's not annoying
because we barely notice it. Through
the years, our hearts and mind goes
through changes–people come and go.
Children grow to become their own.
We wake up to the day that the sound
is stronger–we hear it clearer. Our age
doesn't suppress the sound anymore.
We look back and realize this sound
has always been there, growing louder,
with us. Now we understand it. It's the
sound of life slowly ticking away to a
higher pitch until it fades back with us,
to the end.

We should always say,
'*thank you*',
when we awaken to see,
another day.

I'm feeling more like myself these days,
because I'm thinking less of you,
as I watch you slowly fade away.

Do not underestimate me,
I am even more powerful,
alone.

The embers of the fire in me are floating away like the fireflies on a summer's day.

Live in the moment,
forever,
enjoy.

At times I feel nothing,

other times I feel everything.

Who am I now?

I don't really know.

Am I to the point in life where I am done?

Is there no more for me?

I know I want more, but don't know how

to get there.

I see my days growing longer,

and my nights shorter.

I am numb, but want to feel again.

I want to feel everything,

not nothing.

Thank you.

Embers of the fire

r.j. blonde